A Note to Parents and

DK READERS is a compelling reading pro[...]
children. The programme is designed in conjunction with
leading literacy experts, including Cliff Moon M.Ed., who
has spent many years as a teacher and teacher educator
specializing in reading. Cliff Moon has written more than
60 books for children and teachers. He is series editor to
[Co]llins Big Cat.

Beautiful illustrations and superb full-colour photographs
combine with engaging, easy-to-read stories to offer a fresh
approach to each subject in the series. Each DK READER is
guaranteed to capture a child's interest while developing his
or her reading skills, general knowledge, and love of reading.

The five levels of DK READERS are aimed at different
reading abilities, enabling you to choose the books that
are exactly right for your child:

Pre-level 1: Learning to read
Level 1: Beginning to read
Level 2: Beginning to read alone
Level 3: Reading alone
Level 4: Proficient readers

The "normal" age at which a child begins to read can be
anywhere from three to eight years old. Adult participation
through the lower levels is very helpful for providing
encouragement, discussing storylines and sounding
out unfamiliar words.

No matter which level you
select, you can be sure that you
are helping your child learn to
read, then read to learn!

LONDON, NEW YORK, MUNICH,
MELBOURNE, AND DELHI

Editors Rachel Wardley,
Steve Setford, and Lara Tankel
Designer Andrew Burgess
Senior Editor Linda Esposito
Deputy Managing Art Editor Jane Horne
Production Siu Chan
Picture Researcher Angela Anderson
Illustrator Peter Dennis
Jacket Designer Natalie Godwin
Publishing Manager Bridget Giles

Reading Consultant
Cliff Moon, M.Ed.

Published in Great Britain by
Dorling Kindersley Limited
80 Strand, London WC2R 0RL

Copyright © 2010 Dorling Kindersley Limited
A Penguin Company

4 6 8 10 9 7 5 3
005-177247-Mar/2010

A CIP catalogue record for this book
is available from the British Library

ISBN: 978-1-40535-248-2

Colour reproduction by Colourscan, Singapore
Printed and bound in China by L. Rex Printing Co. Ltd.

The publisher would like to thank the following for
their kind permission to reproduce their photographs:
Key: c=centre; t=top; b=bottom; l=left; r=right
Andes Press Agency 38tl, 41tr (Caretas); **Archivo Fotografico** 15t;
Barnaby's Picture Library:F Newman 45t; **The Bridgeman Art
Library** 14b; **Andrew Burgess** 7cl; **Camera Press** 4 tl, 20b; **Circus
World Museum** 23b; **Colorific!**:Penny Tweedie 5bl, 43t;
Corbis-Bettman:Reuters 45b; **Corbis-Bettmann**:UPI 4 bl 22t 27t, 28,
29, 31t, 34t 35b, 36tl, 37tr, 41br; **Mary Evans Picture Library** 4cr, 9t,
15cl 16-17b, 22b, 30tr, 31b, 33bl; **Robert Harding Picture Library**
4cl, 14t (Guy Motil); **Hulton Getty** 33tr, 26t; **Library of Congress**
30-1b; **Picture Works**:Ingrid Morejohn 18b, 20t; **Pictor
International** 26b; **Planet Earth Pictures** 4 br, 23tl, 24cl; **Rex
Features** 19m; **Science Photo Library**: NASA 32 cl; **South
American Pictures**: Tony Morrison 38cl; **Frank Spooner Pictures**
5cr (Brian Morrison). 46tr (Bouvet/Hires/Duclos) 46b (Fornaciari

DK READERS

EARTHQUAKES
AND OTHER
NATURAL DISASTERS

Written by Harriet Griffey

A Dorling Kindersley Book

Floodwater
Torrential rain can cause river-banks to burst.

Planet power!

Volcanoes, earthquakes, tidal waves, hurricanes, flash floods and forest fires – nature running wild is both spectacular and terrifying.

Despite all our modern resources, natural disasters still devastate lives.

Long Island, USA
(Hurricane, 1938)
Fierce storm winds whipped up huge waves and ravaged the eastern coast of the United States.
See pages 32–37.

Lisbon, Portugal
(Earthquake, 1755)
Earth tremors and fires devastated Portugal's capital.
See pages 14–17.

NORTH AMERICA

PACIFIC OCEAN

ATLANTIC OCEAN

EUROPE

AFRICA

SOUTH AMERICA

San Francisco, USA
(Earthquake, 1906)
The city was shaken to the ground and then consumed by fire.
See pages 26–31.

Yungay, Peru
(Avalanche, 1970)
In the mountains of Peru, an avalanche of ice and rock buried the people of Yungay alive.
See pages 38–41.

Martinique, Caribbean
(Volcano, 1902)
The terrible eruption of Mount Pelée destroyed the port of St. Pierre.
See pages 22–25.

Every year millions of people are killed, injured or left homeless.

Here are the stories of some of the worst natural disasters in history. The map below tells you where the disasters occurred and where you can find them in this book. ❖

Hurricane winds
These winds can rip trees from the soil, toss cars around as if they were toys, and tear roofs off buildings.

Pompeii, Italy
(Volcano, 79 CE)
Mount Vesuvius erupted, burying the Roman town of Pompeii under layers of ash and mud.
See pages 6–13.

ASIA

INDIAN OCEAN

AUSTRALIA

Yellow River, China
(Flood, 1887)
The Yellow River flooded China's Great Plain, killing two million people
See pages 18–21.

Lava flow
Red-hot lava may ooze gently from a volcano or be thrown high into the air by the force of the eruption.

Southern Australia
(Bushfire, 1983)
A severe drought caused fires to rampage across the Australian bush.
See pages 42–45.

Vesuvius
Farmers grew crops on Vesuvius. They had no reason to fear the volcano – it had been quiet for 800 years.

Take-away
At outdoor cafés, snacks were served from bowls sunk into the counter.

Vesuvius erupts!

ITALY, 79 CE

It was a scorching-hot morning. At the foot of Mount Vesuvius, an inactive volcano in southern Italy, the Roman town of Pompeii baked in the August sunshine.

Despite the heat, Pompeii's streets and markets were bustling. The smell of fresh bread from bakers' ovens filled the air, and travelling musicians entertained the shoppers.

At a take-away restaurant, two women ordered snacks for their children. A man tied his dog to the counter and waited to be served.

In the packed taverns, people spoke excitedly about the afternoon's games in the amphitheatre. This was a stadium where huge, bloodthirsty crowds gathered to watch trained warriors called gladiators fight each other – often to the death!

Just then, the ground trembled. The women at the take-away counter exchanged worried glances. Could it be another earthquake? They were common in the area but usually did little damage.

Suddenly there was a deafening boom – and the top of Mount Vesuvius blew right off!

Gladiator helmet
Gladiators were criminals or slaves. The most successful fighters were granted their freedom.

Amphitheatre
Gladiator fights and chariot races were held in Pompeii's amphitheatre.

Blast-off!
Hot, liquid rock moved up through the volcano until it blasted through the top of the mountain.

Unlucky wind
The force of the eruption broke the hot rock into billions of pieces of ash. Wind blew the deadly ash cloud towards Pompeii.

Mount Vesuvius was erupting! A fountain of fire shot upwards and huge black clouds rose into the sky. The ground shook with the force of the explosion. People staggered, clinging tightly to one another.

The eruption of Vesuvius was similar to this 1980 eruption of Mount St. Helens in Washington State, USA.

The women at the take-away restaurant pulled their children close. The dog barked wildly and strained at its lead. Taverns emptied and people ran from their homes, afraid to stay indoors in case the buildings collapsed.

Although it was daytime, darkness fell on Pompeii as ash and smoke blocked out the sun. Lightning bolts zigzagged through the towering cloud of ash above Vesuvius.

Smouldering ash and rocks – some the size of tennis balls – rained down from the sky. Crowds ran screaming through the gloomy streets, upsetting market stalls and trampling fruit and vegetables underfoot. Even gladiators training in the amphitheatre dropped their weapons and ran.

Some people rushed to save precious objects. Others tied cushions or towels to their heads for protection as they fled the streets of Pompeii.

Eye-witness
A man named Pliny watched the eruption from a distance. This description of the explosion is based on his account of the disaster.

Raging sea
The water in the nearby Bay of Naples boiled as hot rocks and ash fell on its surface.

Hot ash stuck in people's throats and made their eyes water. In no time at all, their clothes were coated in a thick layer of ash. As quickly as they brushed it off, a new layer formed!

Everyone was terrified. One man shouted, "The gods are angry with us! It's the end of the world!"

Another man prayed to the gods for help, wailing, "Have mercy on us!"

The ash piled up deeper and deeper. Soon it blocked the streets like a snowdrift. It filled rooms and caused roofs to cave in. The air became so thick with ash and choking fumes that it was impossible to breathe. The town was quickly disappearing under what looked like a blanket of grey snow.

About 2,000 people either chose to stay or were trapped in Pompeii. All of them died. Most of them suffocated or were crushed to death by falling buildings. But as many as 20,000 people managed to escape to the surrounding countryside.

In less than two days the town was buried under 4.5–6 metres (15–20 feet) of ash and rocks. Heavy rain set the ash hard like cement. The town of Pompeii then lay sealed in its rocky tomb for the next 1,800 years.

Roman gods
The Romans worshipped many gods and goddesses. Venus (above) was Pompeii's main goddess.

Volcanic ash
The eruption of Vesuvius threw ash so high into the air that it landed as far away as Africa and Syria!

Burned toast
Eighty-one loaves of bread (cooked and ready to be eaten that day in 79 CE) were found in a baker's oven.

In 1860, the king of Italy ordered archeologists to uncover Pompeii. As they dug away the layers of rock, they were amazed to find the town almost exactly as it was when the volcano erupted – a pile of coins lay on the counter of a tavern, pots and pans stood on a hearth, a bowl of eggs had been placed on a table.

They also found that the bodies of the Pompeiians had rotted away and left hollow shapes in the rock.

This dog lies curled up in agony, still wearing his bronze collar and chain.

This cast shows a mother trying to shield her child from the ash.

The archeologists poured wet plaster into the hollows to make models of the bodies, called casts. When the plaster had set hard, the archeologists chipped away the surrounding rock and removed the casts. Many of them show people shielding their faces, clutching bags of jewels or huddled together in terror.

The eruption of Vesuvius was a terrible event. But so many people and things were frozen at the moment of their destruction that today we have a priceless record of how the Romans lived at that time.

Mount Vesuvius is still an active volcano. It has erupted forty times since 79 CE – in 1631, 18,000 people died. The most recent eruption was in 1944. Who knows when it will decide to wake up again? ❖

Pompeii today
Today, it is possible to walk along the streets of ancient Pompeii.

Scary reminder
This picture of a skull is from a house in Pompeii. The skull was meant to remind people to enjoy life while they could.

Lisbon's great quake

PORTUGAL, 1755

Lisbon
This is Lisbon today. In 1755 275,000 people lived in the city. It was the centre of Portugal's empire, which stretched to South America.

Galleons
These huge ships brought precious cargoes such as gold, silver, silk and spices from all over the empire.

All was peaceful in Lisbon, the capital city of Portugal. Mighty ships called galleons were moored in Lisbon's harbour, their cargoes safely delivered. The streets were nearly empty. Most people were in church for the festival of All Saints Day, when worshippers remember loved ones who had died.

In the royal chapel, King José and his family bowed their heads in prayer. Candles burned steadily on the altar, and the smell of incense filled the air.

Suddenly there was a menacing rumble. Then another, lasting two full minutes, shook the city. It was the unmistakable shuddering of an earthquake! Church spires swayed like corn in a breeze. Inside the churches, bells clanged and chandeliers swung crazily.

Buildings tottered and then crashed to the ground, crushing the people inside.

A third tremor threw clouds of dust into the air, adding to the chaos and confusion. As the royal chapel began to crumble, the king and his family rushed outside. Hordes of people were running to the harbour to escape the falling buildings. But even there, they were soon to discover, they would not be safe.

King José I
José was king of Portugal between 1750 and 1777.

Giant waves
The giant waves that struck Lisbon's harbour were 15 metres (50 feet) high.

Destruction
Buildings that survived the quake were then gutted by flames.

When the crowds reached the harbour, they watched in horror as shock waves from the earthquake pulled the sea back one kilometre (half a mile). Then the sea reared up and returned in three giant waves that smashed ships onto the shore and swept away the terrified onlookers.

Fire raced through the city as overturned candles set alight wooden beams from collapsed buildings. Soon the city was a raging inferno. Lisbon was almost destroyed.

King José and his family escaped unharmed. But 60,000 people died and only 3,000 of the city's 20,000 houses were left standing.

The disaster in Lisbon attracted interest from scientists. They suggested that earthquakes were natural events caused by movements inside the Earth and not divine anger. ❖

Poor peasants
Peasants own land but are poor. They work the land, growing crops and herding their animals.

Yellow River
The river snakes through northern China to the Yellow Sea. Its name comes from the colour of the clay it carries.

River of Sorrow

NORTHERN CHINA, 1887

Life was tough for the Chinese peasant farmers who lived beside the mighty Yellow River. No matter how hard they worked each day in the fields below the river, they barely produced enough food to feed their families.

Over the centuries, the Yellow River had flooded the flat lands of China's Great Plain more than 1,500 times. The river had claimed so many lives and caused such tremendous suffering that it was known as "China's Sorrow".

September 1887 was a month of almost continuous rain. The river began to rise and people feared that it would burst its banks.

Despite the threat of flooding, no one thought to leave. It was their home and their families had lived there for hundreds of years. And it was harvest time – they would starve if they did not bring in their crops soon.

The rain continued to fall and the river rose higher and higher. In some places the river was already 5 metres (15 feet) higher than the flat lands that lay below its banks. While some peasants gathered in the harvest, others set to work building embankments, or dykes, alongside the river. These dykes were their only hope of holding back the water.

But it was no use. At a sharp bend near the city of Zhengzhou, the fast-flowing river finally swelled over its banks. It tore a one-km (half-mile) -long gap in the dykes, pouring a torrent of water onto the Great Plain.

Harvest crops
The peasants grew wheat, corn, rice, sweet potatoes and a type of grass called sorghum.

Flood defence
For 2,500 years the Chinese have built dykes and dug channels to take away the floodwater.

19

Rafts
The peasants' straw and wicker rafts were similar to those used on the Yellow River today.

Disease
Drinking water that was contaminated by the flood led to disease.

Constant threat
The river has often flooded since 1887. In 1991, 1,270 drowned and 2,000,000 were left homeless.

The flood swept away the peasants in the fields but their cries could not be heard above the noise of the rushing water. As the torrent reached the villages beyond the river, people climbed onto their roofs for safety. Some braved the flood in boats or rafts, rescuing people or throwing food to those marooned by the raging water.

The flood covered 11 cities and 1,500 villages and killed 900,000 people. Thousands more died of disease and starvation. It took 18 months to fix the dykes and bring the river back under control.

Today, the flood defences along the Yellow River are much better. Dynamite has been used to alter the river's course to avoid dangerous bends, and huge, powerful dams have been built. But the river will never be completely tamed. "China's Sorrow" will surely claim many more victims. ❖

Pelée awakes

MARTINIQUE, CARIBBEAN, 1902

Mount Pelée
This mountain was named after Pele, the Hawaiian goddess of volcanoes. A minor eruption 50 years before had covered the mountain with grey ash.

It was nearly 8:00 a.m. and the port of St. Pierre on the Caribbean island of Martinique was bustling. Sugar, rum and bananas were being loaded onto ships, while rich French tourists strolled along the elegant streets. Local people toiled in the heat of the orchards and plantations.

Yet people were leaving town. Some were waiting for boats to take them off the island. Others were leaving by road. They were nervous because the usually quiet Pelée was belching smoke and ashes.

At night, red-hot cinders from Mount Pelée lit up the sky.

An official report had said there was no danger. But this did not stop the fear that gripped the town and Governor Mouttet sent guards to stop more people from leaving.

Leon, the local shoemaker, watched the people leaving. He had lived here all his life and knew there was no cause for alarm.

In his jail cell, Auguste Ciparis wasn't concerned either. Locked away, without even a window, he knew nothing of events in the town.

23

Stopped watch
This watch melted to a stop at 8:15 a.m.

Bloodthirsty
The harbour at St. Pierre filled with hungry sharks attracted by the dead bodies floating in the water.

Suddenly Mount Pelée exploded with a sound like a thousand cannons firing. A glowing cloud of white-hot steam, dust and gas rolled down the mountain – heading straight for St. Pierre!

The suffocating air killed most people instantly. Some tried to escape but they were overtaken by the rapidly moving cloud. It was so searingly hot, some of the people's skulls and stomachs burst open.

Leon staggered into his house, clutching his chest. His lungs were racked with pain and his skin was burning. He threw himself onto his bed, expecting to die. All around him things began to melt in the heat.

The streets ran with burning rum from flattened warehouses. Ships in the harbour capsized and sank as the fiery blast swept over them. In a matter of seconds, St. Pierre was reduced to a flaming ruin!

Glass wine bottle

Melting
Temperatures reached 1,000°C (1,800°F), melting objects like the wine bottle above.

Iron nails

Amazingly, Leon survived. But rescuers found no one else alive. Then, after four days, a faint cry was heard. Digging hard, they found Ciparis buried in the rubble of the prison. The thick walls of his cell had saved his life! He was later pardoned and granted his freedom.

The eruption of Pelée was the 20th century's worst volcanic disaster. Only two people survived. The rest of St. Pierre's 30,000 citizens were wiped out in a few minutes. ❖

Spoon and fork

San Francisco
The city began as a shanty town and grew rich from the gold rush of the mid 1800s.

Chinatown
Many Chinese labourers lived in Chinatown. They formed the largest Chinese community outside of the Far East.

Earthquake!
SAN FRANCISCO, USA, 1906

Dawn was breaking over the city of San Francisco. Two tourists named Carl and Pedro were strolling back to their hotel after enjoying the night-life in the city's Chinatown district.

The two friends were joking and chatting about the evening's fun. "What a night we've had!" said Pedro, laughing. Suddenly, Carl seemed to hurl himself against a wall. "Hey! Stop fooling around!" shouted Pedro. Then he, too, was thrown off-balance as the earth shook and heaved beneath his feet.

Bricks and broken glass showered down as buildings began to tilt and sway. "It's a quake, it's a quake!" cried a terrified man as he ran past.

Screams could be heard above the loud rumbling and grinding of the earthquake, as people fled from their collapsing houses. Most were still dressed in their pyjamas.

The tremors only lasted a few minutes. Carl and Pedro looked around and saw that whole streets had been flattened by the earthquake. Even City Hall, which was supposed to be shockproof, had been shaken to pieces.

City Hall
The dome of the hall was left standing on a skeleton of girders.

Tremors
The main
earth tremor
lasted one
minute and
five seconds.

**Ham and
Eggs Fire**
One of the
worst fires was
the "Ham and
Eggs Fire". It
began when a
woman cooked
breakfast in
her shattered
home.

Fire trucks
The city's
38 horse-
drawn fire
engines were
no match for
the 52 fires that
broke out in
San Francisco.

Earthquakes were nothing new to the people of San Francisco. The city sits on the San Andreas Fault, a great crack in the Earth's surface. Two chunks of the Earth's skin meet at this fault. These chunks, called plates, slide against each other, sometimes causing earthquakes.

Carl and Pedro returned to their hotel but found only a heap of rubble. All the other guests had been crushed to death when it collapsed.

But the danger had just begun. Gas from broken pipes filled the air. Fires started as the flames from stoves and heaters, and sparks from severed electricity cables, ignited the gas. Soon whole streets were ablaze.

The water mains had shattered, too, so there was no water supply. Without water, the firefighters had to battle the blazes with sewage. Restaurant owners broke open bottles of wine to dampen the flames.

Firefighters blew up entire streets with dynamite, trying to create fire breaks – gaps between buildings to stop the flames from spreading. But the fires raged on.

Fire breaks
Efforts to stop the fires by blowing up buildings simply created more fires.

The fires destroyed more buildings than the earthquake.

Looters
Thieves picked through the rubble for valuables. Some thieves were shot on sight by police.

Finally the fires died out. Only 500 people had been killed, but 200,000 people were left homeless. They slept on the streets or in Golden Gate Park, building shelters from whatever they could find. Some women gave birth to their babies on the grass in the park!

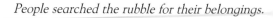

People searched the rubble for their belongings.

Rebuilding began immediately. Within four years, there was barely a trace of the quake's destruction.

Earthquakes still rock the city – a 1994 quake killed 61 people. But buildings are now constructed to withstand the tremors and firefighting techniques have improved. San Francisco no longer has to be rebuilt after each earthquake. ❖

Makeshift stoves
People prepared their meals on temporary stoves until the electricity was restored.

Camps
Thousands of people lived in tents for up to three years after the earthquake.

Long Island Express

NORTHEASTERN USA, 1938

"Forecasters from the US Weather Bureau are warning that a hurricane is heading towards Florida," said the report on the radio in Janice Kelly's Long Island home.

Janice heard the report but her mind was on other things. Long Island, on the north-east coast of the USA, was a long way from Florida. She was thinking about the rats that were scuttling around in her basement. Janice hated rats! She would not be able to relax until her husband got rid of them.

Down in Florida, people started boarding up their houses. Hurricanes were a common occurrence. But as they worked, the hurricane changed direction. At first it seemed to be heading out to sea, where it would cause no harm. Then it turned north.

Wind speed
The hurricane travelled at 96 kph (60 mph), but wind speeds inside it reached 290 kph (180 mph).

Storm-free
Long Island had not had a hurricane for 100 years.

Gathering pace, it raced towards Long Island and the New England states like an express train. When it struck, it took everyone by surprise – toppling skyscrapers and demolishing homes as if they had been crushed by a giant steam-roller!

Flying houses
In Madison, Connecticut, one house was lifted up and blown one kilometre (half a mile) and yet not a single window was broken!

People fled from falling buildings, dodging the flying bricks.

Windy city
The force of the hurricane winds in New York was so strong that it caused the Empire State Building to sway.

The first place hit was Long Island. Families were relaxing on the beach, enjoying their picnics and watching their children build sandcastles. Out at sea, the wind was whipping up huge waves. People who lived along the shore invited their friends to come and look at the big breakers.

Suddenly a wall of water 12 metres (40 feet) high rose up just off shore and crashed onto the beach, sweeping everyone away.

The sea surged inland, flooding towns along the coast. People were tossed about in the floodwaters. Some were rescued by those in higher buildings, who let down bedsheets and hauled them to safety.

Hurricane winds blasted across seven states, derailing trains and splitting roads. Floodwaters set off car horns. Their blaring added to the screams of the raging winds.

Toppled train
This train was surrounded by sea-water and began to sink. Luckily, all the passengers escaped.

Flood damage
This road split into two when floodwater loosened the soil beneath it.

Wave power
In some places, the force of the waves changed the shape of the coastline permanently.

Destruction
The winds and
the tidal wave
they produced
destroyed
more than
57,000 houses.
About 275
million trees
were felled.

Janice Kelly and her husband clambered onto the roof of their house to escape the rising water. They were not the only ones to seek refuge on the roof. Three rats and a snake had beaten them to it! Janice shuddered. She hated rats! But the raging storm terrified her even more.

Then, with a loud ripping sound, the wind tore the roof off the house! It swirled away across the bay, with the couple still clinging on. They closed their eyes, expecting to die.

Suddenly they jolted to a halt. They had come to rest on a golf course.

The Kellys looked across the bay to where their house once stood. Houses were flattened, cars were overturned and half-buried in mud and nearly every tree had been uprooted. The roof had been a miraculous life raft for the Kellys and their bedraggled animal passengers!

The hurricane devastated thousands of lives. Sixty thousand people were left homeless. The final death toll stood at more than 600. The "Long Island Express", as it was named, cut a path 523 km (325 miles) long before it finally blew itself out. ❖

Paint stripper
The force of the wind scratched the paint off cars and stripped painted houses down to the bare wood.

Sea-salt
Wind carried sea-salt 193 km (120 miles) inland, where it turned windows white.

Andes
This huge wall of mountains stretches along the entire Pacific coast of South America.

Peru's people
Peruvians are descendants of the ancient Inca people.

Rising higher
The Andes range is rising due to movements inside the Earth. It may one day be the highest in the world.

Avalanche

Peru, South America, 1970

It was the end of May and a group of Japanese friends were on a climbing holiday in Yungay. The town was a small but flourishing tourist resort that sat at the foot of towering Mount Huascarán in the Andes mountains of Peru. The locals, like most of football-mad Peru, were in the grip of World Cup fever. They had high hopes for the Peruvian team.

Each day the Japanese friends set off early to watch the sun rise over the Andes. At night, they sat under the 30-metre- (100-foot-) tall palm trees in the town square and listened to the excited chatter of the townsfolk.

One afternoon, while the friends were out climbing, a tremendous earthquake split apart the ocean bed just off the Peruvian coast. Earth tremors rippled right across mainland Peru.

It struck 23 minutes into the first World Cup game. Most of the locals were at home, following the match.

High up on Mount Huascarán, the Japanese climbers paused to enjoy the scenery. As they looked down at the quiet town, a low rumbling began. It seemed to grow louder and louder.

Then, far beneath them, the mountainside started to move. As they watched in horror, a huge mass of ice and rock cascaded down the face of the mountain. It was heading right towards the town!

Speed
An avalanche can move three times faster than motorway traffic!

Boulders the size of houses hurtled down the mountain, part of a deadly wall of ice, mud and rock. As the climbers watched, the wall hit the town and buried it.

The climbers hurried down to look for survivors but Yungay had been wiped away. All that remained visible were the tops of four of the palm trees in the town square. The only survivors were a few people who had taken refuge in a hilltop cemetery at the edge of town.

Yungay was just one of many towns and villages devastated by the earthquake. The whole world was shocked by the scale of the disaster.

A short time later, Peru won its World Cup match against Bulgaria. The success helped lift the people's spirits as they began the long task of rebuilding their shattered lives. ❖

Rescue
It was three days before the mud was hard enough for outside help to get to Yungay.

This statue of Jesus in the cemetery was the only thing not destroyed by the avalanche.

Bushfire

AUSTRALIA, 1983

It was the hottest February on record. In some parts of southern Australia it hadn't rained for four years. The wild country known as the bush was as dry as a bone. Koalas sheltered in eucalyptus trees and kangaroos searched in vain for water.

On a farm near the city of Melbourne, Alan and Judy Watts looked at their scorched fields. "I'm worried," said Judy. "There have been fire warnings on the radio all day."

Out in the bush, the dry vegetation began to smoulder and then catch fire in the sun's intense heat. Fanned by the wind, the small fires grew rapidly. Trees began bursting into flames.

Firefighters and groups of volunteers called "bush brigades" fought to control the raging fires.

Bush
The bush is uncultivated land covered with scrub and trees.

Eucalyptus
These trees burn quickly because they have oil-filled leaves.

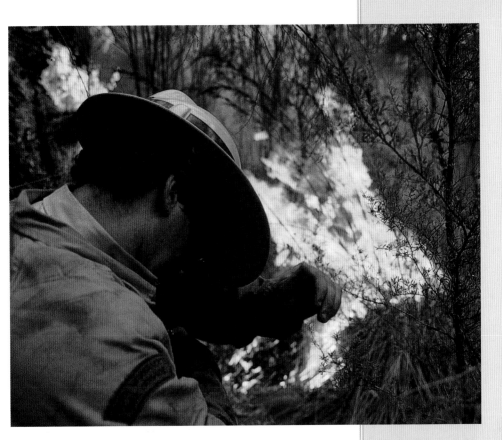

But soon a wall of fire 15 metres (50 feet) high was rolling over the land, reaching speeds of more than 113 kilometres (70 miles) per hour!

The Watts family saw the dark, dusty smoke heading towards them. In no time at all their home seemed to be surrounded by a towering wall of flames. Huge fire balls jumped across the farm road. There was no escape!

Bush brigades
These firefighters carry water packs and spade-like beaters to put out the flames.

Ash clouds
In Melbourne, ash from the fire formed a thick crust over swimming pools.

"We've only got one chance – get in the water tank now!" shouted Judy. As the flames bore down upon them, they scrambled into the huge water-storage tank near the house. Standing in the water, they listened to the terrifying crackle of the fire as it stripped the forest of its trees. The raging fire made the water hotter and hotter, until it was almost unbearable. "We're going to be boiled alive!" thought Alan.

Finally the fire passed by and the water began to cool. After ten hours, the Watts family hauled themselves out of the tank. Dazed and

exhausted, they peered through the smoky air. Their house was gone. Hundreds of farm animals lay dead on the blackened land. The Watts couldn't believe they had survived.

Charred earth
The fires left 60,702 hectares (150,000 acres) of land looking like a war zone.

At least 70 other people were not so lucky. A family of five died in their car as they tried to race away from the flames. Twelve firefighters were engulfed in flames. The fire caused devastation. It destroyed seven towns and left 8,500 people homeless. The relentless flames also killed more than 200,000 cattle and sheep, as well as countless kangaroos and koalas. It is the worst bushfire in Australia's history. ❖

Refugees
Temporary camps were built to house people left homeless by the fire.

This survivor was rescued after a volcanic eruption in Colombia, 1985.

A microphone allows rescuers to talk to a trapped person.

Dealing with disasters

RESCUE OPERATIONS – A RACE AGAINST TIME

After a big disaster, rescue operations are often difficult and dangerous. Collapsed buildings crush many people to death but leave others trapped under the rubble. Flooded homes leave lots of people stranded. For rescuers, finding survivors is a race against time.

RESCUE EQUIPMENT

Trapped person detector
When thousands of people are buried alive, this machine finds survivors by detecting movement. This equipment helped save hundreds of lives after the Armenian earthquake in 1988.

Thermal image camera
This camera is used after all kinds of disasters. It works by detecting the heat of a living person.

Sniffer dogs
Specially trained dogs help rescuers find survivors buried by mud or rubble.

The controls show if heat is present.

Preparing for Disasters

Living in disaster zones means monitoring volcanoes, fault lines and weather patterns so that people can be prepared. Natural disasters cannot be prevented but good planning can help reduce some of their worst effects.

Shake it up

Buildings in earthquake-prone regions are designed to withstand the deadly shaking. The Transamerica Pyramid in San Francisco looks fragile, but its cone shape makes it sturdier than a square-sided building.

Transamerica Pyramid

Everyday drills

In Japan and California, earthquake drills are part of everyday life. Children learn to keep a torch and sturdy shoes by their bed in case an earthquake strikes at night.

Snow stoppers

Trees planted above a village are the oldest and best way of slowing down avalanches. Another device is a solid V-shaped stone wall, which can divide an avalanche so that it passes around a village or building. ❖

Glossary

Amphitheatre
An open-air stadium.
The ancient Romans
watched gladiators fight
in the amphitheatre.

Archeologist
An expert who digs up
ancient remains and tries
to work out what
happened in the past.

Avalanche
A huge fall of rock, ice
and snow from the side
of a mountain.

Bush
An open, uncultivated
area of grasses, shrubs
and trees.

Cast
A model made by pouring
plaster or molten metal
into a hollow mould.

Crust
The Earth's outer layer,
made up of huge slabs of
rock that rest on a bed
of liquid rock.

Drought
A long period with very
little rain or no rain at all.

Dyke
A wall built alongside a
river or canal to hold
back floodwater.

Earthquake
A shaking of the ground
caused by movement
of the segments, known
as plates, that make up
the Earth's crust.

Eruption
The explosion of a
volcano, which may
throw out lava, steam,
ash, dust, suffocating
fumes and hot gas.

Fire break
A gap that is made by
firefighters in a forest or
between buildings to stop
a fire from spreading.

Forecaster
A scientist who studies
the weather and predicts
how it will change.

Galleon
A large sailing ship with
three or four masts.
Galleons were used from
the 15th to the 18th
centuries as warships and
trading vessels.

Gladiator
A trained fighter in the
ancient Roman empire,
who battled against other
gladiators or wild animals
for the entertainment of
the Roman citizens.

Governor
A person who rules a
place on behalf of
another country.

Hurricane
A terrible storm with a
swirling mass of powerful
winds at its centre.

Incense
Special sticks that are
burned for the fragrant
fumes they give off.

Lava
Red-hot liquid rock from
inside the Earth that
bursts on to the surface.

Looters
People who steal things
from a disaster scene.

Monsoon
The rainy season in
tropical regions.

Natural disaster
A destructive event
caused by the forces
of nature.

Plain
A large expanse of level
land in the open country.

Plates
Segments of the Earth's
crust. These large slabs
of rock cover the Earth's
surface like a giant
jigsaw puzzle.

Skyscraper
A tall building consisting
of many storeys, usually
built of concrete and steel.

Tremor
A trembling of the
ground. Earthquakes are
usually made up of a
number of powerful
tremors, coming one
after the other.

Volcano
A mountain with a
central crater through
which hot gases, ash and
molten rock sometimes
burst out.